DINOSAURS

MEET THE GIANTS OF THE **PREHISTORIC WORLD**

PaRragon

Bath • New York • Cologne • Melbourne • Delhi
Hong Kong • Shenzhen • Singapore • Amsterdam

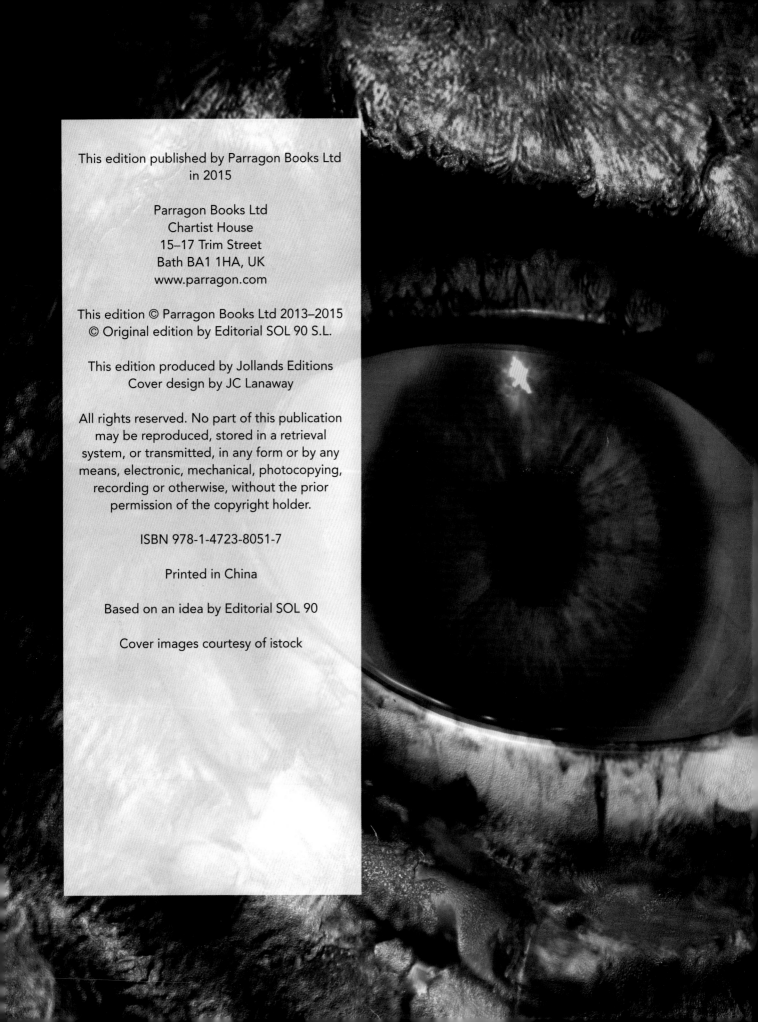

CONTENTS

Introduction

Ever since the first dinosaur bones were brought to light nearly two hundred years ago, people have been fascinated by these extinct creatures. The term 'dinosaur' comes from two Greek words meaning 'terrible lizard'. It was first used in 1842 by the British palaeontologist Sir Richard Owen. Palaeontologists study fossils and other evidence of ancient life to learn about the history of Earth. Every fossil is a clue, and from these they can build up a picture of life in prehistoric times.

Our planet was formed around 4.6 billion years ago. The first living creatures appeared roughly 1.2 billion years later. These organisms developed from single-celled to multicelled organisms, and they gradually moved from rivers and oceans onto dry land.

The dinosaurs existed during a period of time known as the Mesozoic era. At first, they lived on the Pangaea supercontinent, the only landmass on the planet at that time. Gradually their population increased, and they became extremely varied, until they were the most common form of life on land. Enormous herbivores (plant eaters) such as *Brachiosaurus* and powerful predators such as *Giganotosaurus* roamed the land. But by the end of the Mesozoic era, 65 million years ago, there were no dinosaurs left on Earth. Scientists still debate what could have happened to cause this mass extinction.

For a long time, many palaeontologists thought that dinosaurs were slow-moving creatures, with behaviour similar to some reptiles of today. But more recent evidence has suggested that many of the dinosaurs were fast, active creatures that probably lived in groups and travelled long distances. Skin impressions from dinosaurs have also revealed that many of them had feathers. This great discovery was one of the clues that helped to link the dinosaurs with birds. The study of dinosaurs continues to attract the interest of experts and the public alike. Whatever advances are made in the field of palaeontology, there are always many questions that remain to be answered, and there is always something new to find.

BRACHIOSAURUS
A giant herbivore that lived 150 million years ago.

Beginning of Life

Scientists divide time into eras in order to talk about events that have happened throughout history and help understand life on Earth. Eras are then divided into periods, epochs and ages to describe shorter amounts of time.

PRECAMBRIAN ERA

The Precambrian era spanned more than 4 billion years. Its beginning marked the point when the solid crust of the Earth began to develop from liquid rock, known as lava. Then, around 2.1 billion years ago, oxygen started to form in the atmosphere.

PALAEOZOIC ERA

The Palaeozoic era started with an explosion of life in the Earth's oceans. It ended with the biggest destruction of species in Earth's history, when nearly 90 per cent of sea life perished. During this era, reptiles, amphibians and insects developed on land.

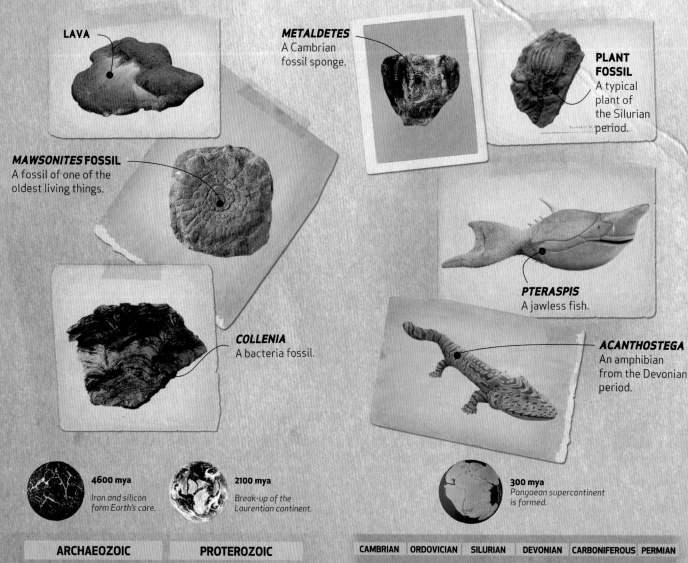

LAVA

METALDETES
A Cambrian fossil sponge.

PLANT FOSSIL
A typical plant of the Silurian period.

MAWSONITES FOSSIL
A fossil of one of the oldest living things.

PTERASPIS
A jawless fish.

COLLENIA
A bacteria fossil.

ACANTHOSTEGA
An amphibian from the Devonian period.

4600 mya
Iron and silicon form Earth's core.

2100 mya
Break-up of the Laurentian continent.

300 mya
Pangaean supercontinent is formed.

ARCHAEOZOIC	PROTEROZOIC
4600–542 mya	

CAMBRIAN	ORDOVICIAN	SILURIAN	DEVONIAN	CARBONIFEROUS	PERMIAN

542–251 mya

mya = millions of years ago

4600 mya
Formation of the Earth

3400 mya
First bacteria (single-celled organisms) appear

2100 mya
Oxygen forms in the atmosphere

700 mya
First multicellular animals

PRECAMBRIAN

PALAEOZOIC

MESOZOIC

CENOZOIC

TIMELINE
For the greatest part of history, organisms with only one cell were the main life forms on Earth. The first organisms made up of many cells (multicellular) appeared 700 million years ago.

MESOZOIC ERA
The Mesozoic era was the time of the dinosaurs. Other reptiles included tortoises, crocodiles, lizards and snakes. Birds, mammals and the first flowering plants also appeared. The era ended with the disappearance of many life forms.

CENOZOIC ERA
The dawn of the Cenozoic era saw the extinction of the dinosaurs. Since then, mammals have dominated, and birds have increased in number. At the very last moment in Earth's long history, human beings appeared.

BAROSAURUS
Huge herbivore (plant eater) that lived 150 million years ago.

GIGANOTOSAURUS

BAROSAURUS BONE

TITANIS
One of the first birds.

THYLACOSMILUS
A sabre-toothed marsupial.

AUSTRALOPITHECUS AFARENSIS
A human ancestor.

AUSTRALOPITHECUS
A human ancestor.

200–180 mya
Break-up of Pangaea into continents. Africa, India and America separate.

60 mya
Continents are already similar to present-day landmasses, and mountains are being formed.

TRIASSIC	JURASSIC	CRETACEOUS		TERTIARY	QUATERNARY

251–66 mya

From 66 mya to present times

What is a Dinosaur?

Dinosaurs were animals that appeared about 230 million years ago. They evolved into an amazing variety of shapes and types: some giants, others small; some herbivores, others carnivores. They had horns, crests and bony plates as protection, and many had feathers. The dinosaurs disappeared in the Cretaceous period but left behind descendants with feathers that could fly – birds.

Dinosaurs are usually described as reptiles, but they looked different from tortoises, lizards or crocodiles because of their body posture. Their limbs grew downwards from their bodies, not out from their sides, as in most reptiles. Their posture was straighter, and they were able to move faster and more gracefully than other reptiles. Many species of dinosaurs could rise onto their rear legs and use their toes when walking or running. This more efficient way of moving was one of the keys to the dinosaurs' success against the competition of other reptilian species.

Many dinosaur species reached gigantic sizes. *Argentinosaurus* and *Puertasaurus* are considered the largest land animals ever. They reached almost 35 m (115 ft) from the tip of their nose to the end of their tail. But not all dinosaurs were huge. There were some species that were the same size as chickens, such as *Scipionyx*, found in Italy, *Microraptor* from China and *Ligabueino* from Argentina.

TAIL
A long and robust tail was used to balance the weight of the body.

NECK
This part of the body became S-shaped.

TYRANNOSAURUS REX
One of the largest land carnivores of all time.

LEGS
The structure of the legs and hips was similar to that of present-day birds.

THE EVOLUTION OF REPTILES

As dinosaurs evolved from reptiles, the main changes were related to movement, from reptilian to bipedal (two-footed) forms.

1 REPTILIAN

In lizards, the limbs spread outwards, with elbows and knees bending, and the belly dragging on the ground.

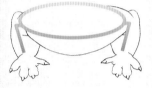

2 SEMI-ERECT

In crocodiles, the limbs stretch outwards and downwards, with elbows and knees bent at an angle of 45 degrees. Crocodiles crawl when moving slowly and straighten their legs when running.

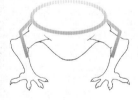

3 BIPEDS

In dinosaurs, the rear limbs were straight beneath the body, so that the body was never dragged, not even when the dinosaur was walking very slowly.

Classification

This chart shows the relationships between the groups of dinosaurs, starting from the main divisions (Saurischia and Ornithischia), when they first evolved from early reptiles in the Triassic period. Over the next 160 million years they evolved into many different groups.

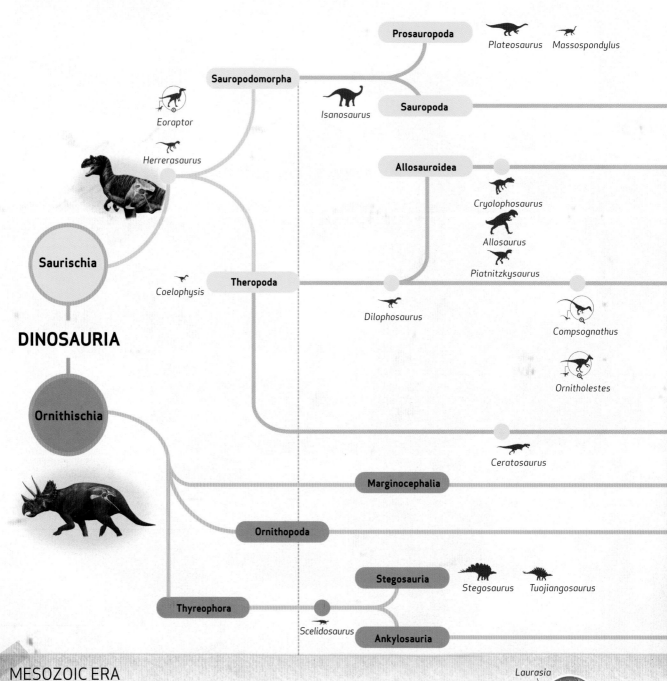

Prosauropoda

Plateosaurus *Massospondylus*

Sauropodomorpha

Eoraptor

Isanosaurus **Sauropoda**

Herrerasaurus

Allosauroidea

Cryolophosaurus

Allosaurus

Piatnitzkysaurus

Saurischia

Coelophysis **Theropoda**

Dilophosaurus *Compsognathus*

DINOSAURIA

Ornitholestes

Ornithischia

Ceratosaurus

Marginocephalia

Ornithopoda

Stegosauria

Stegosaurus *Tuojiangosaurus*

Thyreophora

Scelidosaurus **Ankylosauria**

MESOZOIC ERA

TRIASSIC Dinosaurs appeared in this period, 230 million years ago. They lived together with other reptiles.

JURASSIC 150 mya Gigantic herbivores appeared, along with powerful carnivores. At the end of this period, the first birds developed.

Laurasia

Gondwana

NAMING

Scientists arrange living organisms into related groups. The names of these groups help us know the category and position of the organism. This is done by changing the ending (suffix) of each name. For example, the suffix used for superfamilies is '-oidea' (Tyrannosauroidea), and the one for families is '-idae' (Tyrannosauridae). When we refer to a family of dinosaurs in English we add '-ids' (tyrannosaurids).

Diplodocus

Diplodocoidea

Amargasaurus

Brachiosaurus

Mamenchisaurus

Titanosauroidea

Argentinosaurus *Saltasaurus* *Rapetosaurus*

Megaraptor *Giganotosaurus* *Carcharodontosaurus*

Spinosauroidea

Ornithomimosauria

Deinocheirus *Gallimimus*

Therizinosauria

Baryonyx *Suchomimus* *Spinosaurus* *Beipiaosaurus*

Therizinosaurus

Oviraptorosauria

Scipionyx *Caudipteryx*

Alvarezsauridae

Sinovenator

Troodontidae

Birds

Patagonykus

Archaeopteryx *Sinornithosaurus*

Microraptor

Dromaeosauridae

Unenlagia *Velociraptor*

Eotyrannus **Tyrannosauroidea**

Tyrannosaurus

Abelisauroidea

Carnotaurus *Masiakasaurus*

Pachycephalosauria

Pachycephalosaurus

Psittacosaurus **Ceratopsia**

Zuniceratops *Protoceratops* *Triceratops*

Hypsilophodontidae

Gasparinisaura

Iguanodontidae

Iguanodon *Ouranosaurus* *Muttaburrasaurus*

Minmi

Hadrosauroidea

Corythosaurus

Edmontonia

CRETACEOUS
100 mya

Dominant groups evolved and new species appeared. All of them disappeared at the end of this period.

India *Eurasia*

South America *Antarctica*

Anatomy Characteristics

Fossils of dinosaur skeletons, teeth, footprints, eggs and skin have given us huge amounts of information about the different kinds of dinosaurs. Palaeontologists piece this information together with data about the dinosaurs' environment and present-day species to build up a picture of the anatomy (body structure) of dinosaurs.

We know from the many fossilized dinosaur skeletons that have been found that dinosaurs looked very similar to reptiles. Their bone structure, the scales that covered their bodies and their birth from shelled eggs are key similarities.

Dinosaurs, however, had many features that were different from their reptile relatives, such as adaptations in their legs and hips, as they developed from crawling to a more upright posture. During this process, a new arrangement of muscles evolved.

Most of the information we have about the body structure of dinosaurs comes from their bones, as these hard parts fossilized best. In a very few cases, impressions of dinosaur skin have been found in the fossils. From these we know that some dinosaurs had hard coverings and small scales, while some recently discovered dinosaurs had feathery coverings. The study of present-day birds and reptiles also helps us to reconstruct the body posture of dinosaurs.

Ossified tendons (flexible cords that have changed into bone-like material)

Tibia (shin bone)

DEINONYCHUS SKELETON

The main features of the carnivorous dinosaur *Deinonychus* were similar to those of other theropods: a large skull, a short and curved neck, a strong backbone, and hind legs much longer than the front ones.

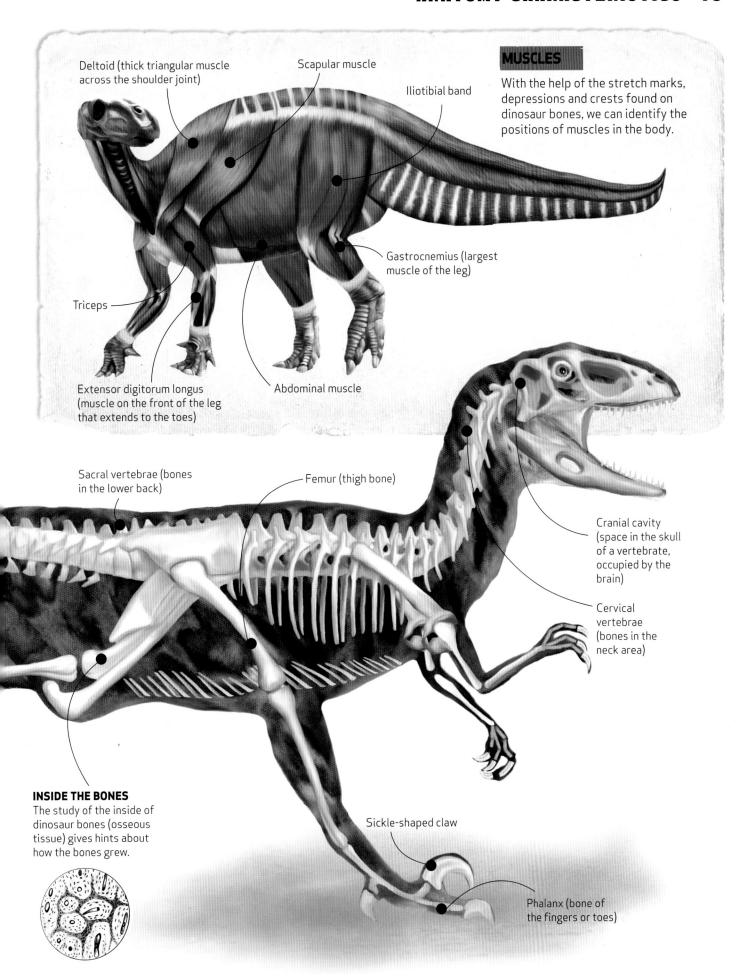

Deltoid (thick triangular muscle across the shoulder joint)

Scapular muscle

Iliotibial band

MUSCLES

With the help of the stretch marks, depressions and crests found on dinosaur bones, we can identify the positions of muscles in the body.

Triceps

Gastrocnemius (largest muscle of the leg)

Extensor digitorum longus (muscle on the front of the leg that extends to the toes)

Abdominal muscle

Sacral vertebrae (bones in the lower back)

Femur (thigh bone)

Cranial cavity (space in the skull of a vertebrate, occupied by the brain)

Cervical vertebrae (bones in the neck area)

INSIDE THE BONES
The study of the inside of dinosaur bones (osseous tissue) gives hints about how the bones grew.

Sickle-shaped claw

Phalanx (bone of the fingers or toes)

Inside a Dinosaur

CENTRAL CONTROL

The brains of herbivores were smaller than the brains of carnivores. A dinosaur's brain was located and protected inside the skull, just like ours, and different nerves pointed outwards to collect information from the eyes, nose, mouth and ear openings. The spinal cord started from the brain and extended through the backbone.

SIZE COMPARISON

TYRANNOSAURUS
Tyrannosaurus had a brain smaller than that of humans.

STEGOSAURUS
Stegosaurus had a brain the size of a walnut.

TROODON
Troodon's brain was similar in size to that of *Tyrannosaurus rex*, but because it was large in relation to its head, it is thought to have been a more intelligent dinosaur.

SIZE AND WEIGHT

Dinosaurs were a group of animals with a very wide range of sizes. Some dinosaurs, such as *Epidexipteryx*, were as tiny as sparrows, while *Argentinosaurus* still holds the record for the largest land animal ever.

SIZE
Many dinosaurs were small in size.

Basset hound

Velociraptor

WEIGHT COMPARISON
African elephant (5,400 kg/12,000 lb) = 15 *Protoceratops*

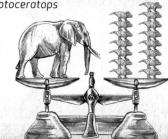

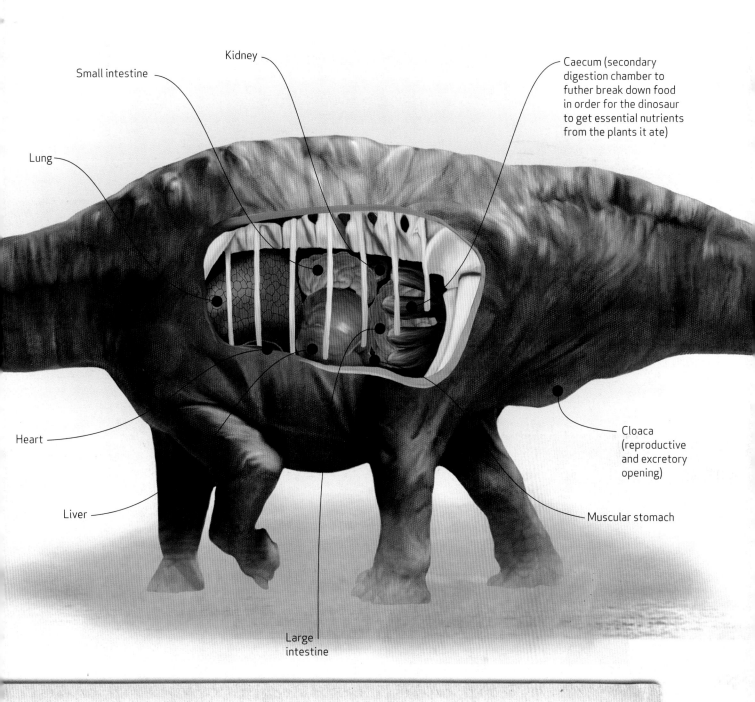

Kidney

Small intestine

Caecum (secondary
digestion chamber to
futher break down food
in order for the dinosaur
to get essential nutrients
from the plants it ate)

Lung

Heart

Liver

Cloaca
(reproductive
and excretory
opening)

Muscular stomach

Large
intestine

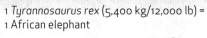

1 *Tyrannosaurus rex* (5,400 kg/12,000 lb) =
1 African elephant

1 *Argentinosaurus* (80,000 kg/180,000 lb) = 15 African elephants

The World of the Dinosaurs

Towards the end of the Triassic period, as many ancient reptiles became extinct, dinosaurs took their place, and in the Jurassic period the largest living creatures ever to roam the land fed on the abundant vegetation. By 100 million years ago there were dinosaurs of many sizes; in the air, pterosaurs flew alongside birds and small insects such as bees and moths.

D inosaurs grew to huge sizes in the Jurassic. Sauropods (plant-eating dinosaurs) such as *Brachiosaurus* were among the largest. Alongside them were smaller, faster species that may have hunted in groups. *Archaeopteryx*, the first known bird, appeared towards the end of the Jurassic. It shared the skies with flying reptiles that had been on the planet since the Triassic.

In the oceans, ichthyosaurs and plesiosaurs lived with big sea crocodiles, sharks, rays and cephalopods (molluscs with tentacles, such as octopuses), similar to those alive today. Sea levels rose during the Cretaceous, when there were no ice caps covering the poles, and much of the land was covered with warm, shallow water.

There was an explosion of different life forms, including mammals and insects, and the dinosaurs continued to develop in many varied forms. These included horned species like *Triceratops*, and giant carnivores such as *Tyrannosaurus rex*.

VEGETATION
Empty zones were soon covered up with trees.

PLANTS

Plants such as ferns and horsetails, as well as different species of coniferous trees, formed thick forests. Flowering plants appeared around 100 million years ago.

Araucaria

Conifers

FORESTS
Forests flourished in areas with warm, humid climates, and gradually spread to other areas.

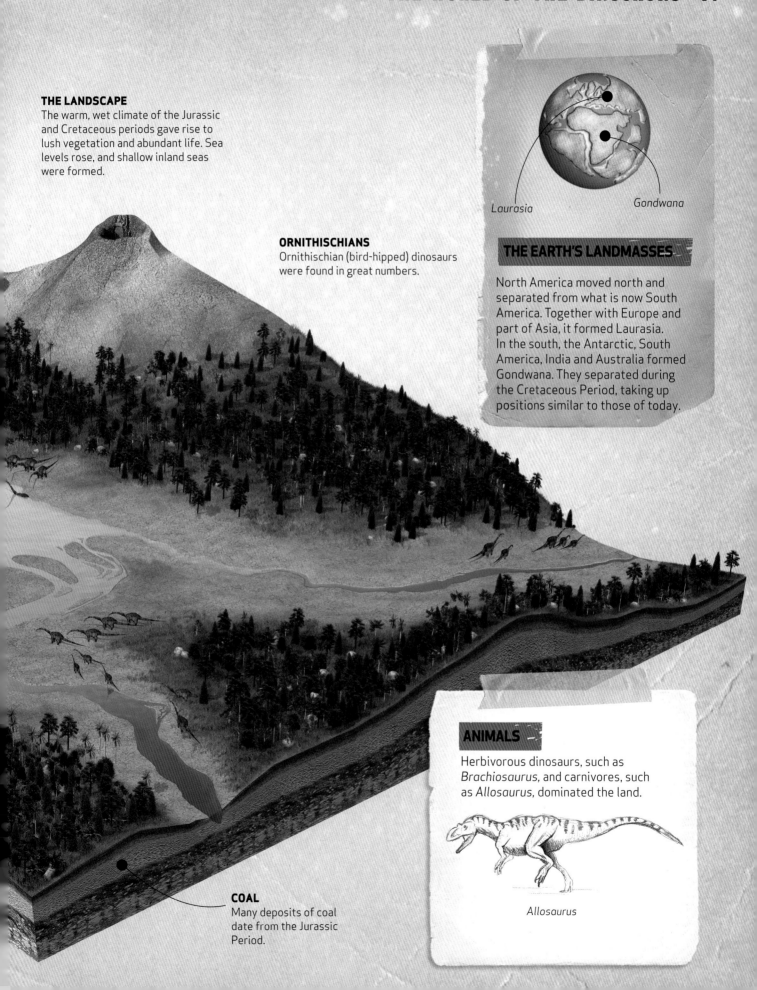

THE LANDSCAPE

The warm, wet climate of the Jurassic and Cretaceous periods gave rise to lush vegetation and abundant life. Sea levels rose, and shallow inland seas were formed.

ORNITHISCHIANS

Ornithischian (bird-hipped) dinosaurs were found in great numbers.

Laurasia

Gondwana

THE EARTH'S LANDMASSES

North America moved north and separated from what is now South America. Together with Europe and part of Asia, it formed Laurasia. In the south, the Antarctic, South America, India and Australia formed Gondwana. They separated during the Cretaceous Period, taking up positions similar to those of today.

ANIMALS

Herbivorous dinosaurs, such as *Brachiosaurus*, and carnivores, such as *Allosaurus*, dominated the land.

Allosaurus

COAL

Many deposits of coal date from the Jurassic Period.

Dilophosaurus

Dilophosaurus was made famous by the 1993 film *Jurassic Park*. Its most notable feature was the double crest in the upper part of its skull.

Dilophosaurus was the largest member of an ancient family of two-legged dinosaurs that lived at the end of the Triassic and beginning of the Jurassic periods. Its remains have been found in Africa, North America, South America, Europe and Asia, showing that it was present in large numbers as the Pangaea supercontinent was being formed.

The ancient relatives of *Dilophosaurus* all had a long, low skull, with many teeth, and a narrow snout. The neck was thin and flexible, which meant it could stretch out quickly to allow the dinosaur to catch prey in its mouth.

Its name means 'two crests reptile', since its most obvious characteristic was the complex structure of crests on its head. They were very thin, and it is thought that they may have been used for communication and recognition, much as cockerels use their fleshy 'combs' today.

At the beginning of the Jurassic period, *Dilophosaurus* was the most dangerous predator because there were no other large carnivores around at that time.

GENUS: DILOPHOSAURUS
CLASSIFICATION: THEROPODA, COELOPHYSOIDEA

LENGTH 6 m (20 ft)
WEIGHT 500 kg (1,100 lb)
DIET Carnivorous

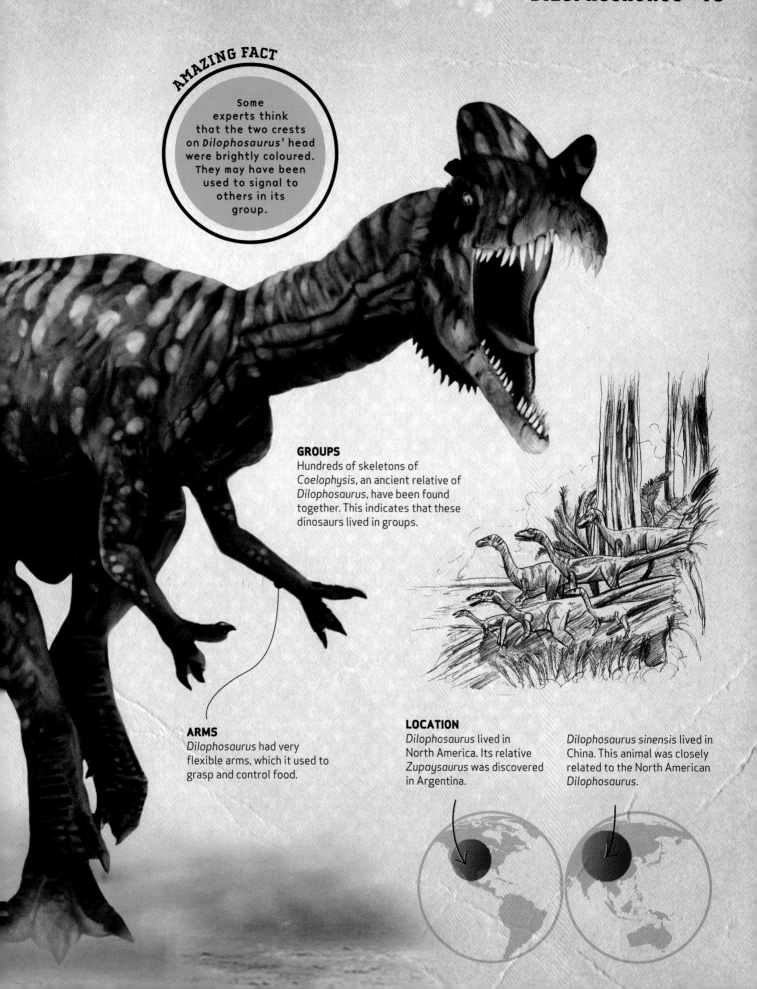

AMAZING FACT

Some experts think that the two crests on *Dilophosaurus*' head were brightly coloured. They may have been used to signal to others in its group.

GROUPS

Hundreds of skeletons of *Coelophysis*, an ancient relative of *Dilophosaurus*, have been found together. This indicates that these dinosaurs lived in groups.

ARMS

Dilophosaurus had very flexible arms, which it used to grasp and control food.

LOCATION

Dilophosaurus lived in North America. Its relative *Zupaysaurus* was discovered in Argentina.

Dilophosaurus sinensis lived in China. This animal was closely related to the North American *Dilophosaurus*.

Dilophosaurus

LONG TAIL
Dilophosaurus had a large number of bones in its tail. The main function of the tail was to balance the body.

HANDS
Dilophosaurus had three fingers with claws and a fourth one that was smaller in size. This set the pattern for the structure of the hands of future theropods.

LEGS
The legs of *Dilophosaurus* were long and muscular. They had three toes facing forward and another smaller one pointing to the side. *Dilophosaurus* ran very fast on its hind legs.

SKULL
The skull was long, with two rounded crests along its centre. There were wide openings for the nasal cavities and eye sockets.

CRESTS
The two delicate crests on the head may have been colourful and were probably used to help animals recognize each other.

Stegosaurus

This armoured dinosaur lived in North America 145 million years ago, but its relatives were found on many different continents. *Stegosaurus* ate low-lying plants that were digested in its massive stomach.

The beginning of the Jurassic period saw the appearance of small two-legged animals called thyreophorans ('shield bearers'). These birdlike dinosaurs had protective body coverings. The best known is *Scutellosaurus*, whose skin was protected by tiny cone-shaped shields. These creatures were the forerunners of the stegosaurs and ankylosaurs, which developed thicker, more complex armour.

The stegosaurs had large triangular plates and spikes along their necks, backs and tails. They were four-legged, with hooflike claws. The most ancient was *Huayangosaurus*, which was about 3 m (10 ft) in length, but *Stegosaurus* reached up to 9 m (30 ft).

Stegosaurs had five toes on their front feet and only three on their back feet. They carried their heads close to the ground, so that they could feed on low-lying plants.

The plates on a stegosaur's back were used in many ways – not just as armour, but also for display and recognition, to communicate with members of the herd, and possibly to regulate the dinosaur's body temperature. At the end of the creature's tail there were two pairs of long spikes, which were probably used as weapons.

The brain cavity in the skull was very small, but there was a large area of spinal cord in the hip area.

This has led experts to suggest that this dinosaur might have had a 'second brain'.

At the beginning of the Cretaceous period, about 130 million years ago, *Stegosaurus* became extinct, possibly because of competition from new plant-eating species.

GENUS: STEGOSAURUS
CLASSIFICATION: ORNITHISCHIA, THYREOPHORA, STEGOSAURIDAE

LENGTH 9 m (30 ft)
WEIGHT 5,000 kg (11,000 lb)
DIET Herbivorous

AMAZING FACT

Some species of stegosaur defended themselves by lashing out with their spiked tails. *Stegosaurus* used its tail as a weapon, striking directly at enemies.

TEETH

Stegosaurus' teeth could bite but were not big or flat enough to chew tough leaves. Instead, the food was swallowed and broken down in the digestive system.

TAIL SPIKES

Spikes at the end of *Stegosaurus'* tail pointed dangerously to the sides.

LOCATION

Stegosaurus fossils have been found in the USA, in rock formations dating from the end of the Jurassic period.

Several types of stegosaur fossils have also been found in layers of rocks from the Jurassic period in Africa, Portugal and China.

Stegosaurus

BACK PLATES
The back plates were wide and thin, with an average height and width of around 50 cm (2 ft).

HIPS
Stegosaurus had features similar to birdlike dinosaurs, with the forward portion of the hip bones pointing downwards and backwards.

SKELETON
The back was curved. The front legs were short, and the head was small and carried close to the ground. The tail was strong and held well above the ground.

Brachiosaurus

The larger and more rounded body of *Brachiosaurus* made it stand out from other enormous sauropods. Its front legs were longer than its rear ones, and its back was curved as a result. This feature gave *Brachiosaurus* a rather strange appearance.

The fossil remains of *Brachiosaurus altithorax* were discovered by Elmer Riggs in 1902, in rocks from the Late Jurassic period in the Morrison Formation in the western USA. The name *Brachiosaurus* refers to its long front limbs, and *altithorax* means 'high chest'.

From reconstructions of the skeleton of *Brachiosaurus* we can see that its front legs were more widely separated than those of the diplodocids, and its chest was very wide. It had powerful muscles that supported and balanced its long, strong neck. Its thick, spoon-shaped teeth suggest that *Brachiosaurus* ate tough vegetation, browsing in the high treetops. Its head may have reached up to 10 m (33 ft) above the ground.

It is thought that *Brachiosaurus* lived in herds and may have travelled long distances in search of food, as elephants do today.

Giraffatitan ('titan giraffe') is the best-known brachiosaur, as many fossils have been found in Tanzania, Africa. It is one of the largest dinosaurs known. Although *Giraffatitan* is a different species from *Brachiosaurus*, it probably had a very similar lifestyle. The arrangement of its teeth would have been very efficient at cropping the Jurassic treetops.

GENUS: BRACHIOSAURUS
CLASSIFICATION: SAURISCHIA, SAUROPODA, MACRONARIA

LENGTH 26 m (85 ft)
WEIGHT 23,000 kg (50,700 lb)
DIET Herbivorous

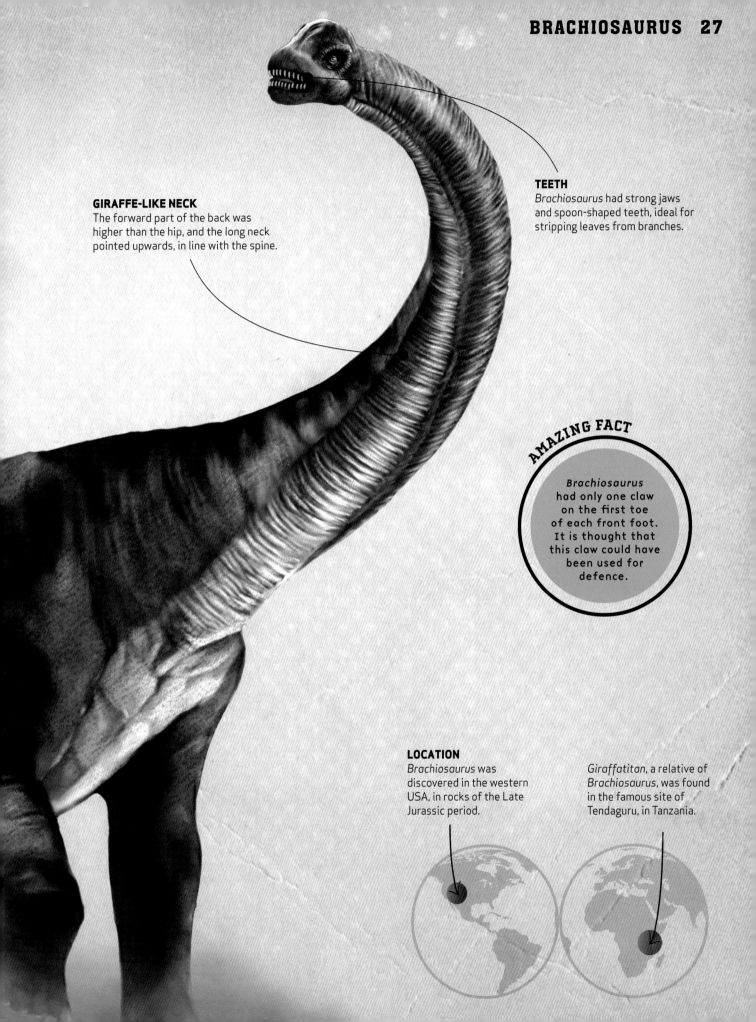

GIRAFFE-LIKE NECK
The forward part of the back was higher than the hip, and the long neck pointed upwards, in line with the spine.

TEETH
Brachiosaurus had strong jaws and spoon-shaped teeth, ideal for stripping leaves from branches.

AMAZING FACT

Brachiosaurus had only one claw on the first toe of each front foot. It is thought that this claw could have been used for defence.

LOCATION
Brachiosaurus was discovered in the western USA, in rocks of the Late Jurassic period.

Giraffatitan, a relative of *Brachiosaurus*, was found in the famous site of Tendaguru, in Tanzania.

Brachiosaurus

EATING JURASSIC TREES
An adult *Brachiosaurus* needed to eat up to 180 kg (400 lb) of leaves and shoots every day to maintain its weight.

AMAZING FACT
In the Jurassic period, *Araucarias* (monkey puzzle trees) were the tallest trees. *Brachiosaurus* could raise its head up to 10 m (33 ft) above the ground to reach them.

SHORT TAIL
Brachiosaurus had a short tail. When walking, it held it above the ground.

BACK LEGS
It's unlikely that it could rear up on its back legs to feed: its long neck made this unnecessary anyway.

GIANT STRUCTURE
The neck was raised in a slight curve. The ribcage was enormous and was supported by its strong legs.

Iguanodon

Large numbers of *Iguanodon* fossils have been found in many different parts of the world. From this evidence, we know that they formed groups, roaming together in search of food.

guanodon, meaning 'iguana tooth', was a dinosaur that lived in Europe in the Middle Cretaceous period, about 125 million years ago. It was a large, strong herbivore that moved on either two or four legs, resting its hooflike fingers on the ground.

Adult animals measured around 10 m (33 ft) long, although some could reach up to 13 m (43 ft). The skull was tall with a narrow snout ending in a toothless beak.

Although first found in England in 1822, the most extraordinary discovery of *Iguanodon* remains was in a coal mine at Bernissart in Belgium, in 1878. Bones from almost 38 animals were gathered from this mine, allowing the Belgian palaeontologist Louis Dollo to assemble several skeletons and to learn a great deal more about these spectacular dinosaurs.

The iguanodonts are grouped together within the Ornithopoda category. The name 'Ornithopoda', meaning 'bird foot', comes from the fact that many dinosaurs in this group had three digits, similar to those of birds.

Ornithopod fossils have been found worldwide – even in Antarctica. These animals first appeared in the Middle Jurassic period, reaching their maximum numbers in the Cretaceous period.

There were two main ancestries: the small, light hypsilophodonts and the more developed, large and heavy iguanodonts. The hypsilophodonts were two-legged and could run fast when attacked. They had long tails, with hard connecting tissues to help them balance while running.

GENUS: IGUANODON
CLASSIFICATION: ORNITHISCHIA, ORNITHOPODA, IGUANODONTIA

LENGTH 10 m (33 ft)
WEIGHT 5,000 kg (11,000 lb)
DIET Herbivorous

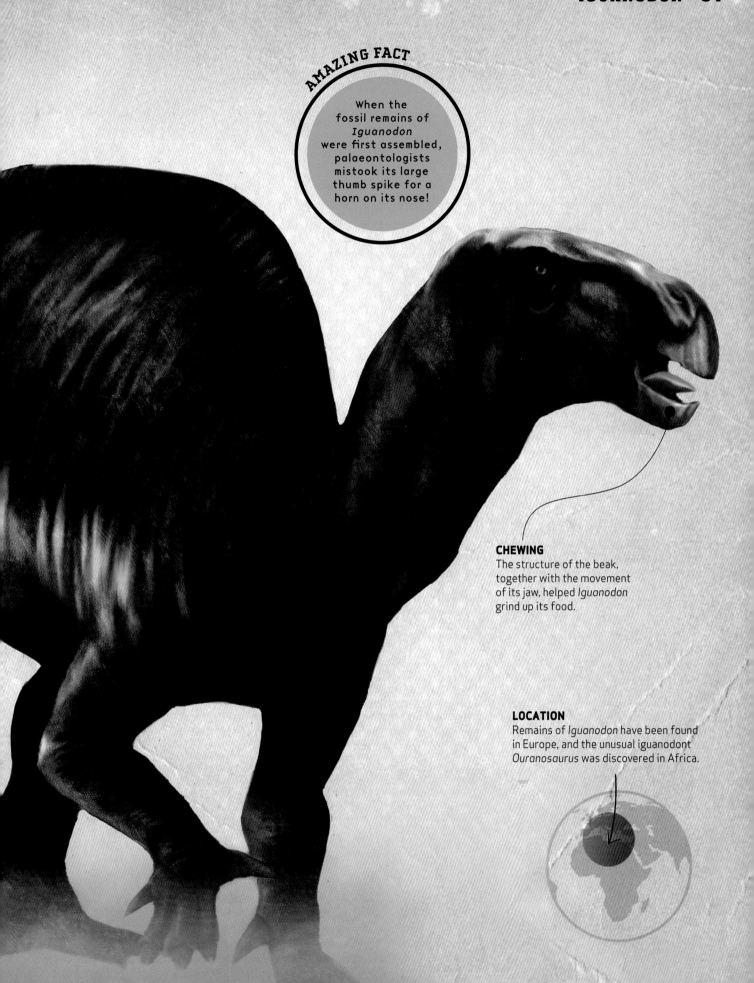

AMAZING FACT

When the fossil remains of *Iguanodon* were first assembled, palaeontologists mistook its large thumb spike for a horn on its nose!

CHEWING
The structure of the beak, together with the movement of its jaw, helped *Iguanodon* grind up its food.

LOCATION
Remains of *Iguanodon* have been found in Europe, and the unusual iguanodont *Ouranosaurus* was discovered in Africa.

Iguanodon

IGUANA TEETH
Iguanodon's teeth were arranged in long rows at the sides of the mouth. Each one of them was similar to a modern iguana's tooth, but much larger.

HANDS
The hands were strong and rigid. A big spike on the thumb was used for defence, while the middle fingers supported the body weight. The outer finger was able to turn back against the other fingers, somewhat like a human thumb.

HIP
The front portion of each hip bone was directed backwards.

LEGS
Iguanodon mainly moved on all four limbs, but it could also run on its two back legs and rear up to reach higher vegetation or fight off rivals and predators.

Giganotosaurus

As its name suggests, *Giganotosaurus* was a gigantic dinosaur – one of the biggest carnivorous dinosaurs ever to have existed. It lived in South America around 90 million years ago.

This 'giant southern reptile' was an enormous predator. It had a large mouth with teeth so sharp that one bite easily slashed through the flesh and muscles of its prey. Its huge body weight and the size of its legs indicate that the animal had a slow and heavy walk, so it could not have run to hunt its prey. However, as it preyed upon titanosaurs, who couldn't run fast either, this was not a disadvantage.

Giganotosaurus belongs to a group of huge theropod dinosaurs known as the carcharodontosaurids, which included perhaps the largest land predators ever known. The oldest known, *Concavenator*, was found in Spain in rocks 130 million years old. This specimen was 6 m (20 ft) long, but some of its later relatives were much bigger.

The name *Carcharodontosaurus* means 'shark-toothed reptile', because these dinosaurs had around 70 very sharp teeth. They could cut through meat, but were probably not strong enough to crunch bones. *Giganotosaurus* and the carcharodontosaurs were some of the main carnivores populating Gondwana between 125 and 90 million years ago. But they mysteriously died out several million years before the massive extinction at the end of the Cretaceous period.

GENUS: GIGANOTOSAURUS
CLASSIFICATION: THEROPODA, TETANURAE, CARNOSAURIA

LENGTH 13.5 m (45 ft)
WEIGHT 8,000 kg (17,500 lb)
DIET Carnivorous

AMAZING FACT

The skull of *Giganotosaurus* was about 1.6 m (5 ft) long. It had one of the largest heads of all the theropods.

LOCATION
Giganotosaurus was found in Cretaceous period rocks in Patagonia, Argentina.

Carcharodontosaurus was found in Egypt, and *Concavenator*, a smaller relative, was found in Spain.

Giganotosaurus

ARMS
It is believed that *Giganotosaurus* had short but strong arms, with three clawed fingers.

SMELL
Its sense of smell may have been sharper than its sight, as it would have been very helpful in detecting prey.

HEAVY LEGS
Giganotosaurus walked on its huge, powerful back legs, which were supported by the central toes of its feet.

Giganotosaurus' tail was powerful and muscly. This helped with balance and allowed it to turn its body quickly and attack suddenly.

Spinosaurus

An extraordinary predator that hunted on land and in water, *Spinosaurus* was one of the most gigantic theropods ever to walk on Earth.

Some palaeontologists believe that *Spinosaurus* was even larger than both *Tyrannosaurus rex* and *Giganotosaurus*. Discoveries made in countries such as Niger, Morocco, Britain and Brazil have provided us with information about the structure and lifestyle of these amazing dinosaurs. Other notable features include a massive skull and rows of spines on the back up to 1.65 m (5.5 ft) long. A recent study has suggested that these supported a large hump of fat, similar to that of a camel. This hump would have stored energy to allow the dinosaur to survive during times when there was little food or water.

The spinosaurids had long snouts and cone-shaped teeth like those of crocodiles. There is plenty of evidence about their feeding habits. The digested remains of fish scales and bones, as well as the remains of a young *Iguanodon*, have been found inside the ribs of fossils of the spinosaurid *Baryonyx*. In Brazil, the mark of a *Spinosaurus* tooth was discovered on a neck bone of a pterosaur. So it's clear that the spinosaurid's diet included fish, young herbivorous dinosaurs and flying reptiles. Like crocodiles, *Spinosaurus* may have had pressure sensors on its snout that helped it detect prey moving in water. This meant that it could strike at fish without being able to see them.

GENUS: SPINOSAURUS
CLASSIFICATION: THEROPODA, TETANURAE, SPINOSAURIDAE

LENGTH 12.5–18 m (41–60 ft)
WEIGHT 5,000–9,000 kg (11,000–20,000 lb)
DIET Carnivorous

LEGS
They were strong enough to support the body weight, which was increased by the extra weight of its spiny back.

AMAZING FACT

Spinosaurus had around 40 teeth, with the largest at the very tip of its long snout; they interlocked like crocodiles' teeth.

LOCATION

Skulls of *Irritator* and *Oxalaia*, one of the largest spinosaurids, were discovered in Brazil.

Baryonyx came from England, and the large spinosaurids *Suchomimus* and *Spinosaurus* from Africa.

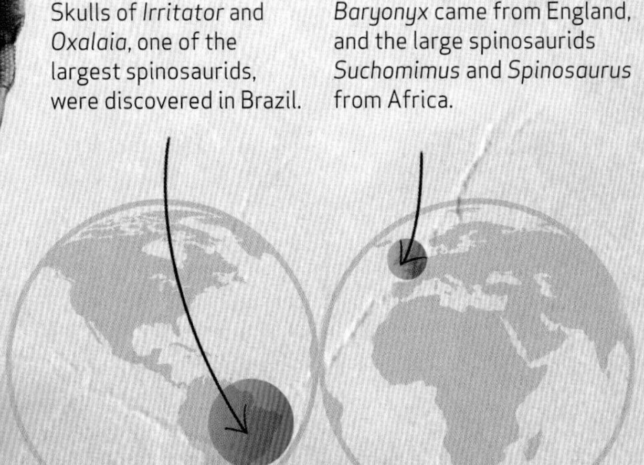

HANDS

The inner finger had a strong, curved claw. It was used as a deadly weapon.

Spinosaurus

LONG HEAD
Spinosaurus' head had a narrow snout with a hooklike tip and many sharp, pointed teeth.

TEETH
The teeth of *Spinosaurus* were cone-shaped and less curved than in other theropods. They are quite similar to the teeth of modern-day crocodiles.

ARMS
Spinosaurus had long, strong arms, very different from those of the tyrannosaurids. The fingers on the hands had highly developed claws.

SPINES
The spines that supported the 'sail' on the back were massive – ten times longer than the diameter of the vertebrae they grew from.

AMAZING FACT

Spinosaurus was probably bigger than *Tyrannosaurus rex*, making it one of the largest carnivorous dinosaurs ever.

Argentinosaurus

Argentinosaurus is one of the largest dinosaurs we know to have existed. The study of this giant has helped us learn more about enormous plant-eating sauropods.

Argentinosaurus huinculensis was named after the Huincul Formation in southwest Argentina, where palaeontologists found its fossil in 1993. Its scientific name means 'Argentinian lizard'. Only parts of the skeleton were recovered, including some vertebrae, ribs, a shin bone and a thigh bone.

were low in nutrients. In order to digest these, sauropods would have needed to keep them in their stomachs and intestines for a long time. As they evolved, their bodies may have grown bigger to fit their enlarged stomachs.

When it was first discovered, *Argentinosaurus* attracted international attention because of its size. Sauropods of similar sizes include *Paralititan*, *Supersaurus*, *Seismosaurus*, *Sauroposeidon*, *Alamosaurus* and *Puertasaurus*, and there may have been even bigger dinosaurs that have not yet been discovered.

The reason for their giant size remains a mystery. One explanation may be the increase in temperatures during the Mesozoic era, as present-day reptiles living near the Equator tend to be larger than those in colder regions. It could also have been the result of feeding on plants that

Argentinosaurus had around 230 bones in its skeleton. However, despite its great length, the neck contained only 13 vertebrae.

BIG BACKBONE
One of *Argentinosaurus*'s vertebrae measures 1.6 x 1.3 m (5 x 4 ft). This gives some idea of the enormous size of this dinosaur.

GENUS: ARGENTINOSAURUS
CLASSIFICATION: SAURISCHIA,
SAUROPODA, TITANOSAURIA

LENGTH 30 m (98 ft)
WEIGHT 73,000 kg
(161,000 lb)
DIET Herbivorous

LOCATION
Argentinosaurus was found near Plaza Huincul, in the southwest of Argentina.

Titanosaurs like *Argentinosaurus* lived during the Cretaceous period in South America, North America, Africa, Asia and Europe.

Argentinosaurus

LONG LEGS
Only a shin bone (tibia) and part of a thigh bone (femur) have been found from the leg. The tibia was 1.5 m (5 ft) long and the femur would have reached up to 2.4 m (7 ft).

AMAZING FACT

From its snout to the end of its massive tail, *Argentinosaurus* may have been as long as three buses lined up end to end.

TAIL
The tail was not as long as in other sauropods. It was very flexible and had more than 30 bones. Its flexibility may have meant that *Argentinosaurus* could rear up on its hind legs better than some of its sauropod relatives.

WEIGHT SAVING
In order to reduce the weight of the skeleton, the inner tissue of the spinal bone was spongy and had huge cavities, surrounded by very thin walls.

Tyrannosaurus rex

Tyrannosaurus rex had a huge head, strong and sharp teeth, and legs well suited for running. This dinosaur was one of the most extraordinary creatures of the prehistoric world.

Tyrannosaurus rex and its close relatives, the tyrannosaurids, evolved in the Northern Hemisphere in the Late Cretaceous period. Skeletons, teeth and footprints of these carnivores have been found in North America and Central Asia.

They were great hunters. Their favourite prey included ceratopsians and hadrosaurs. The larger tyrannosaurids lived alongside the dromaeosaurids (small-sized, fast-running carnivorous dinosaurs).

The strength of *Tyrannosaurus* lay in its huge jaws, powered by muscles in its temples. The shape of the skull hints that it had a good sense of smell, which would have helped it find its prey.

There have been many different theories about the feeding habits of *Tyrannosaurus*. It has even been suggested that it did not hunt at all, but only scavenged for its food. Its hind legs show that it would have been able to pick up enough speed to hunt heavy animals that could not run as fast. Skeletons of *Triceratops* and other hadrosaurs have been found with large teeth marks, thought to have been made by tyrannosaurids. This clue leads us to believe that *Tyrannosaurus* would have been able to capture its prey alive. However, during long periods of drought, it is likely to have scavenged for leftovers.

AMAZING FACT

Tyrannosaurus' arms were much too short to be used to capture prey. The tiny arms were only about the same size as a human's.

GENUS: TYRANNOSAURUS
CLASSIFICATION: THEROPODA, COELUROSAURIA, TYRANNOSAURIDAE

LENGTH 12.5 m (41 ft)
WEIGHT 5,000 kg (11,000 lb)
DIET Carnivorous

TERRIBLE TEETH
Tyrannosaurus teeth were big enough to crunch bones. They had sawlike edges for cutting through flesh.

POWERFUL FEET
Each foot had three strong toes, used to force prey against the ground. There was also a fourth toe, called a 'dewclaw', higher on the foot, but this was almost useless.

LOCATION
Tyrannosaurus rex fossils have been found in the USA and Canada, along with other tyrannosaurids, including *Daspletosaurus*, *Gorgosaurus* and *Albertosaurus*.

Tyrannosaurid fossils have even been found on the other side of the world in Asia, including that of *Guanlong*, a primitive tyrannosaurid from the Jurassic period.

Tyrannosaurus rex

FEATHERED BABY
A baby *Tyrannosaurus rex* probably had feathers, similar to hair, which were gradually lost as it developed.

AMAZING FACT
With huge jaws and teeth up to 23 cm (9 in) long, experts think that *Tyrannosaurus rex* could devour about 225 kg (500 lb) of meat in a single bite.

BIG HUNTER
It is thought that, because of its strength, *Tyrannosaurus* could bring down large herbivores.

LEGS
Tyrannosaurus' legs were long and muscular. Despite their weight, scientists believe that these huge dinosaurs could still run to chase their prey.

HUGE HEAD
The head was 1.4 m (4.5 ft) in length, and it had between 50 and 60 teeth in its mouth.

ARMS
They were so small that *Tyrannosaurus* couldn't even reach its own mouth.

Pachycephalosaurus

Pachycephalosaur means 'thick-headed reptile', and it is probable that these dinosaurs used their tough heads to defend themselves.

Pachycephalosaurus may be one of the most extraordinary looking dinosaurs, with its domed skull and cone-shaped growths. It was two-legged, with long, strong hind legs and short front limbs. Its hips were wide, indicating that it had a large stomach that was able to contain and digest lots of vegetation.

The narrow beak at the end of the mouth had teeth of different shapes. At the upper tip of the snout, the teeth were cone-shaped and good for biting, whereas the ones at the sides of the cheek were leaf-shaped with sawlike edges. It is thought that pachycephalosaurs used their heads as powerful weapons in fights. Their strong necks could withstand the impact of head-on collisions or sideswipes.

Pachycephalosaurs are closely related to the ceratopsians, so they are part of the Marginocephalia group. Dinosaurs in this group all have a skull with an outgrowth over the back of the neck. In ceratopsians, this consisted of delicate neck frills, but in pachycephalosaurs, it was a series of cone-shaped knobs.

During the last 20 million years of the Cretaceous period, dinosaurs of this group evolved in North America and Asia. *Pachycephalosaurus* and *Stegoceras* appeared in the western USA, and *Homalocephale* and

Prenocephale in the Gobi Desert of Mongolia. *Pachycephalosaurus* was the largest member of Marginocephalia. The dome of its skull increased in height as the animal grew to adulthood, and in males it was taller and more curved than in females.

Pachycephalosaurus' eyes were set inside large, deep cavities, which protected them during fights. The muscles of the neck were very powerful, and the backbone was built to withstand impacts. Its widely set hips helped the animal keep its balance.

TAIL
Pachycephalosaurus had a very thick tail with a mesh of tissues at the end to increase its strength.

GENUS: PACHYCEPHALOSAURUS
CLASSIFICATION: ORNITHISCHIA,
MARGINOCEPHALIA,
PACHYCEPHALOSAURIA

LENGTH 4.5 m (15 ft)
WEIGHT 450 kg (990 lb)
DIET Herbivorous

TEETH
They were small but sharp to cut tough plants and leaves.

ARMS
Its front limbs were a lot shorter than the back legs. Each one had five fingers ending in claws.

LOCATION
Pachycephalosaurus was identified in rocks from the end of the Cretaceous period in the western USA.

Several species of pachycephalosaurs have been found in Cretaceous period rocks from Mongolia.

Pachycephalosaurus

SKULL
The skull was attached to the spine and neck with very strong muscles and tendons. This added strength must have been important to *Pachycephalosaurus*, but scientists are still unsure exactly why.

HIPS
The hips were wide, which has led some scientists to believe that these dinosaurs fought each other sideways on.

LEGS
The shape of the bones show they were able to run fast and crash against an enemy.

AMAZING FACT

The rounded skull of *Pachycephalosaurus* was up to 25 cm (10 in) thick. Inside it was a tiny brain.

Triceratops

Triceratops horridus ('three-horned face') lived in North America during the last three million years of the Mesozoic era.

Triceratops was described for the first time in 1889, and since then, hundreds of examples have been found, including specimens of both young and mature animals. This dinosaur fed on low, tough plants that it cut with its powerful beak and chewed with its abundant teeth. It walked on all four legs, and could not raise itself up on its hind legs. The front limbs had three toes and the back legs four, all with rounded hooves.

Triceratops had a short horn above its nostrils and two long horns above its eyes. Underneath, the long horns were part of the bone structure of the skull, but the bone was covered by the horn material.

Like all ceratopsians, *Triceratops* had a large outgrowth of bones at the back of the skull, which protected the soft neck area. Research suggests that it used its horns as defensive weapons against predators, such as *Tyrannosaurus rex*. However, in dinosaurs such as *Styracosaurus* they were fairly thin, so they wouldn't have been strong enough to actually fight with.

Skulls have been found of both young and adult *Triceratops*. The young animals had already developed horns and neck frills, but as they grew older, the horns grew in length and thickness. The bony neck plate grew backwards and became thinner.

GENUS: TRICERATOPS
CLASSIFICATION: ORNITHISCHIA, MARGINOCEPHALIA, CERATOPSIA

LENGTH 9 m (29 ft)
WEIGHT 12,500 kg (26,500 lb)
DIET Herbivorous

Both the horns and the neck plates may have helped *Triceratops* parents to recognize their offspring, since each dinosaur would have had small differences in the size and shape of their horns and neck frills. They may also have been used to show dominance among other *Triceratops*, and to help the animal find a mate.

NECK PLATE
The huge skull was around 2.5 m (8 ft) long, and the rear part pointed backwards to form a protective neck covering.

BEAK JAWS
Triceratops had powerful jaws that were tipped with a pointed beak.

LOCATION
Triceratops has been found in North America. It is unknown in other parts of the world.

Distant relatives of *Triceratops* have been found in Asia, most of them without horns.

Triceratops

THREE-HORNED FACE
The name *Triceratops* means 'three-horned face'. As well as its horns, *Triceratops* had many small spikes along the edge of its neck frill.

TEETH
Triceratops' teeth were arranged in groups called 'batteries'. The largest animals could have had up to 800.

AMAZING FACT

Triceratops always walked on all four legs and had a short tail since it was not needed for balancing.

FRONT LEGS
The powerful front legs supported the weight at the front of the body and provided extra strength when attacking enemies.

Corythosaurus

Corythosaurus lived in large flocks in present-day Canada. It was a hadrosaur, or 'duck-billed' dinosaur, and its remains were found in rocks over 76 million years old.

American palaeontologist Barnum Brown gave *Corythosaurus* its name because its crest looked like the helmet of a Corinthian (ancient Greek) soldier. He found the first skeleton of *Corythosaurus* in the west of Canada. The skeleton that was uncovered was nearly complete; some fossilized skin was even preserved on one side.

Hadrosaurs formed the most successful herbivorous group at the end of the Cretaceous period, mainly in North America and Asia, although fossils have been found in many parts of the world. They had long snouts, somewhat like ducks' bills, and large numbers of teeth grouped in batteries that they used to crush and grind vegetation. The most ancient hadrosaurs were the size of horses, but their descendants from the late Cretaceous period grew to up to 10 m (33 ft) in length.

We know about the hadrosaurs' diet from skeletons with preserved, fossilized plant remains in their stomach area. There are also fossilized faeces, which show that their diet included leaves, fruits and seeds.

The skull of *Corythosaurus* was notable not only for the long snout but also for its large nose. The nostrils were lined with tissues that produced moisture and helped trap particles from the air as *Corythosaurus* breathed.

The hadrosaurs are divided into two families: those with hollow crests, such as *Corythosaurus*, are known as lambeosaurines. In the lambeosaurines, the nasal passages extended into the head crests. Palaeontologists believe that by blowing air through the hollow passages in these crests, lambeosaurines could make loud sounds that would have carried over large distances. They probably helped to keep groups of the animals together and to warn of predators.

LENGTH 10 m (33 ft)
WEIGHT 4,000 kg (8,800 lb)
DIET Herbivorous

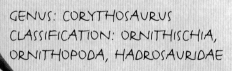

GENUS: CORYTHOSAURUS
CLASSIFICATION: ORNITHISCHIA, ORNITHOPODA, HADROSAURIDAE

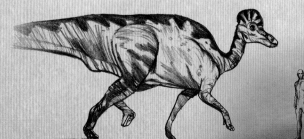

CRESTS
The many species of hadrosaur can be distinguished by the different structures of their crests.

AMAZING FACT

Corythosaurus grazed on low-growing plants, but could also rear up on its hind legs to eat leaves and fruits from trees.

LOCATION
Hadrosaurs lived in large numbers in North America, but *Corythosaurus* has been found only in Canada.

Asia was home to many different hadrosaurs. Among them was *Aralosaurus*, one of the lambeosaurines (hadrosaurs with crests).

FOOT STRUCTURE
Corythosaurus had three thick toes that ended in wide hooves. These helped the dinosaur to walk on all types of terrain.

Corythosaurus

SKIN
The skin of *Corythosaurus* was covered by scales, spread evenly all over the body.

BEHAVIOUR
When feeding, *Corythosaurus* might have joined other herbivorous dinosaurs. These dinosaurs lived in herds and possibly moved regularly from one area to another.

CREST SIZES
The crest sizes would have varied depending on the gender and on the age of the animal.

AMAZING FACT

Although the forelimbs were relatively short, resembling arms, the study of their footprints indicates that *Corythosaurus* walked mainly on four legs.

Origin of Birds

The origin of birds has been much debated. Many palaeontologists today believe that birds are related to flesh-eating, two-legged dinosaurs. The two groups have similarities in bones, feathers, eggs and behaviour. The most detailed studies point to maniraptorans (a group that includes oviraptors) being the direct ancestors of birds.

REPTILIAN INHERITANCE

Maniraptors and theropods have a lot of physical similarities to birds that can be seen on the skeleton.

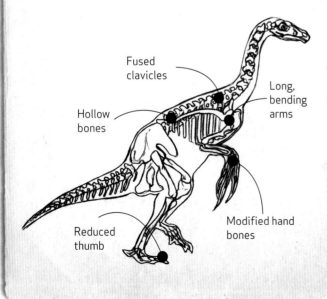

Fused clavicles

Hollow bones

Long, bending arms

Reduced thumb

Modified hand bones

INCUBATING

Some oviraptorid skeletons have been found on top of nests. This proved that dinosaurs sat on their eggs to provide warmth and to help them hatch.

CHICKEN MIMIC
The theropod *Gallimimus* was given its name, meaning 'chicken mimic', because of its birdlike shape – it looked much like an ostrich.

FEATHER COVERAGE
Bones with tiny swellings, found in 2007, show that *Velociraptor* definitely had feathers!

FEATHER EVOLUTION

In the beginning, the purpose of feathers was to maintain body heat. Later on, they became useful for flying.

Growing pimple from inside a pod	Strands appear in the pimple	Branched outgrowths develop	Hooks appear in the outgrowths	Feathers are similar to those of today

 Beipiaosaurus	 *Sinosauropteryx*	 *Sinornithosaurus*	*Caudipteryx*	*Archaeopteryx*

Caudipteryx

Caudipteryx had small, winglike arms with claws. The feathers in its tail balanced the body and were used to identify it to other members of the same species.

Caudipteryx ('tail with feathers') was an oviraptor about the same size as a present-day turkey. It was mainly carnivorous, but it had omnivorous habits – it fed on both invertebrate animals and vegetation. Its head was small and high, with large eyes. It had a short snout with a horny beak and a few tiny, pointed teeth at the end. Some specimens of *Caudipteryx* have gastroliths (stomach stones) in the area of the gizzard, which indicates that it may also have eaten some seeds.

The fossils of this theropod show that its body was covered by short feathers that regulated its temperature. Its arms were covered by longer feathers, but these winglike limbs were not fit for flying. They and the feathers at the tip of the tail helped to balance the body when the animal was running and especially when turning.

The maniraptors ('seizing hands') are the theropods most closely related to birds. Their arms generally bent in a zigzag shape, and had three long fingers ending in curved, pointed claws. A system of tissues and joints made their hands automatically extend forwards when they stretched their arms – a feature shared by birds.

GENUS: CAUDIPTERYX
CLASSIFICATION: SAURISCHIA, THEROPODA, MANIRAPTORA

SPEEDY RUNNER
The long legs, similar to those of a South American rhea, show that *Caudipteryx* was a fast runner.

LENGTH 1 m (3 ft)
WEIGHT 3 kg (6.5 lb)
DIET Omnivorous

AMAZING FACT

AMAZING FACT

As more fossils of feathered dinosaurs and early birds are found, we will understand more about the so-called 'missing link' between them.

DIET
With its narrow beak, *Caudipteryx* caught small invertebrates that it found in the bark of trees.

LOCATION
Maniraptor fossils have been found around the world. *Deinonychus* was discovered in the USA, and *Unenlagia* in Argentina.

Caudipteryx was found in Liaoning, China, together with fossils of other dinosaurs with feathers.

Caudipteryx

NECK
The neck had a large number of bones, making movement easy.

HIND LEGS
Caudipteryx had long, slim legs. It could run quickly when chased by predators.

SKELETON
The skeleton was adapted for swift movement.

Caudipteryx had a small skull. It had large eyes, and a thin snout covered by a hairy beak.

FEATHERED TAIL
The marks on the skin show that the feathers were arranged in a fan shape at the tip of the tail.

Deinonychus

Deinonychus relied on its lethal, sickle-shaped claws for attack and defence. Its name actually means 'terrible claw'.

In 1964, the American palaeontologist John Ostrom and his team discovered around 1,000 *Deinonychus* bones in the western USA. He also found a large number of eggshells underneath adult bones. This indicated that *Deinonychus* provided warmth for its eggs by sitting on them, in the same way that present-day birds hatch their eggs.

    Deinonychus is one of the best-known members of the two-legged, feathered dromaeosauridae family, which appeared in the middle of the Jurassic period and disappeared at the end of the Cretaceous. It was John Ostrom who first drew attention to the noticeable similarities between *Deinonychus* and *Archaeopteryx*, the oldest-known bird. He changed the way palaeontologists thought about dinosaurs, suggesting that they had far more in common with big, flightless birds (such as ostriches) than with reptiles.

GENUS: DEINONYCHUS
CLASSIFICATION: THEROPODA,
COELUROSAURIA, DEINONYCHOSAURIA

LENGTH 3.5 m (11 ft)
WEIGHT 80 kg (175 lb)
DIET Carnivorous

LINHERAPTOR SKELETON
This almost complete skeleton of *Linheraptor*, a close relative of *Deinonychus*, was found in Mongolia.

HUNTER'S ARMS
Deinonychus' arms folded at the sides of its body but could quickly stretch out to capture prey.

LOCATION
In the USA, *Deinonychus* fossils have been found in rocks that are 110 million years old.

In Asia, many deinonychosaurs, including *Microraptor*, *Velociraptor* and *Linheraptor*, have been found.

Deinonychus

TAIL
The bones at the tip of the tail were connected by long, hardened tissues, making it very strong. This helped *Deinonychus* to maintain its balance.

HANDS
Deinonychus had large hands with three long fingers ending in curved claws. These were helpful for grasping and tearing prey.

SHARP VISION
The structure of the bones in the skull allowed both eyes to face forwards, which gave *Deinonychus* good 3-D vision.

SKULL
Deinonychus had strong jaws, with many small, sharp teeth. The snout was narrow, and its bite was very powerful.

AMAZING FACT

Several skeletons of *Deinonychus* were found together in the USA. This suggests that they hunted in groups or gathered together to feed.

Therizinosaurus

Therizinosaurus had a strong body, with long arms and two legs. There was doubt about its classification for years, because of its odd appearance. New finds of complete skeletons show that therizinosaurs were herbivorous theropods.

During the 1940s, palaeontologists from the Soviet Union and Mongolia, working together in the Gobi Desert, discovered some very strange fossils. They were the front limbs of a reptile with amazingly long claws. For decades, the appearance of this animal and its relationship with other dinosaurs remained a mystery. However, the specimens were so large and interesting that eventually the appearance of this mysterious beast was reconstructed.

At first, the remains confused researchers who tried to classlfy them. Russian palaeontologist Evgeny Maleev thought that they belonged to a turtle-like reptile. He gave it the name *Therizinosaurus* ('scythe lizard'). However, new samples found in 1950 showed it was a dinosaur. Several decades after its first discovery, it was classified as a theropod.

Although the known remains of *Therizinosaurus* are incomplete, it has been possible to do a reconstruction of its entire body from studies that compare it with other dinosaurs. It probably had a strong body, with a long neck ending in a small skull. Like the earliest bird-hipped dinosaurs, it moved on two legs, each ending in four toes.

This was different from other known theropods, which had only three toes on their feet.

Therizinosaurus' arms were up to 2.5 m (8 ft) long, with three digits and an enormous claw on each one. It is possible the claws were up to 1 m (3 ft) in length. Some palaeontologists believe they were used as weapons for defence, or in fights for territory. We also know now that *Therizinosaurus* was herbivorous, so it could have used its claws as a tool to cut the branches of trees, as present-day sloths do.

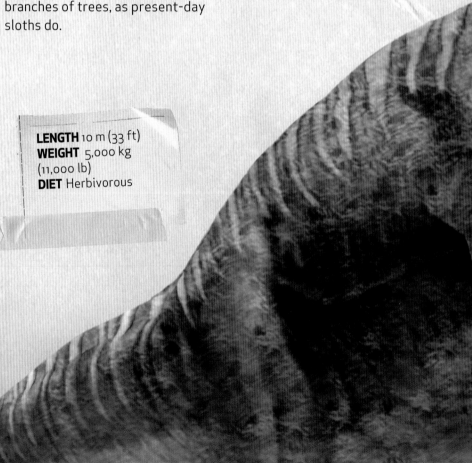

GENUS: THERIZINOSAURUS
CLASSIFICATION: SAURISCHIA,
THEROPODA, THERIZINOSAURIDAE

LENGTH 10 m (33 ft)
WEIGHT 5,000 kg
(11,000 lb)
DIET Herbivorous

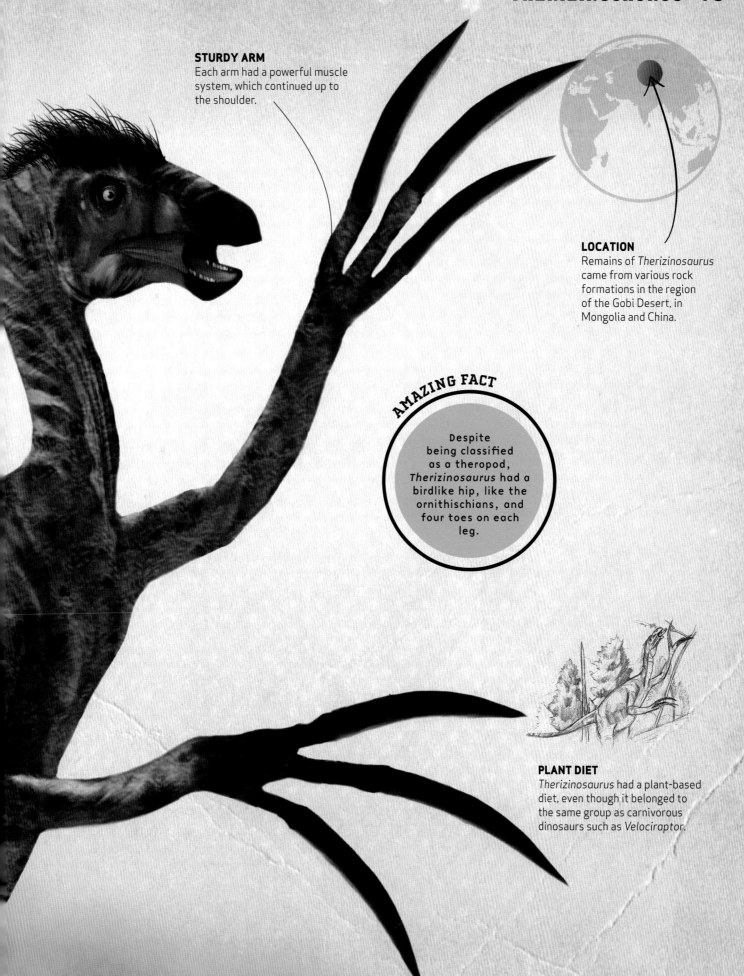

STURDY ARM
Each arm had a powerful muscle system, which continued up to the shoulder.

LOCATION
Remains of *Therizinosaurus* came from various rock formations in the region of the Gobi Desert, in Mongolia and China.

AMAZING FACT
Despite being classified as a theropod, *Therizinosaurus* had a birdlike hip, like the ornithischians, and four toes on each leg.

PLANT DIET
Therizinosaurus had a plant-based diet, even though it belonged to the same group as carnivorous dinosaurs such as *Velociraptor*.

Therizinosaurus

LONG AND SHORT
We know the amazing length of *Therizinosaurus'* arms from the discovery of a complete set of fossil bones. Its legs and tail, however, were short compared to its arms.

SKULL
No fossil skull has been discovered for *Therizinosaurus*, so reconstruction of the head is based on palaeontologists' knowledge of similar dinosaurs.

CLAWS
Therizinosaurus' sharp claws are the longest known claws in any animal.

HIP STRUCTURE
Therizinosaurus had a hip structure similar to that of modern-day birds. It is possible that this shape helped to accommodate its long intestines.

The Mystery of Extinction

Dinosaurs appeared in the Triassic period, taking the place of synapsids and other ancient reptiles. In the Jurassic period, they developed to huge sizes and, in the Cretaceous period, they were widespread and dominant – until they mysteriously disappeared.

The Mesozoic era started 252 million years ago, after a great extinction had removed most of the synapsids from the Palaeozoic era. During the Mesozoic, the most varied, common and gigantic vertebrates were the reptiles. This group included sea animals, land animals, such as dinosaurs and crocodiles, and flying animals, including pterosaurs and birds.

The Mesozoic era finished 66 million years ago in the same way it had started – with a major extinction. The great disappearance at the end of the Cretaceous left the Earth with almost no large animals.

There are many theories to explain why this happened. One of the most popular is that the Earth was struck by a large meteorite. Although nothing has been proved, what we do know for certain is that a catastrophic event caused the disappearance of many species on land and in the sea, bringing to an end the 'golden age' of the reptiles.

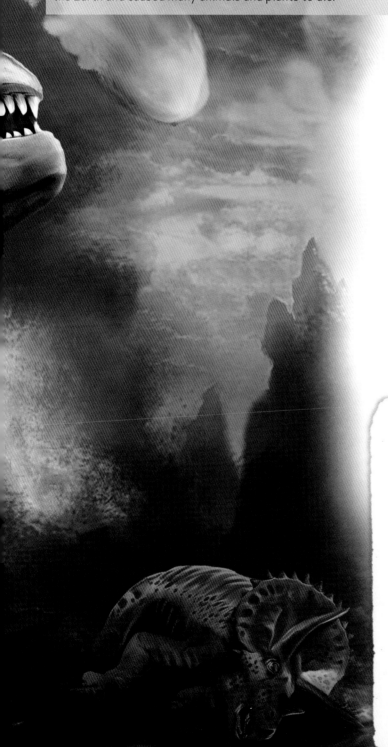

LETHAL IMPACT

It is believed that a large meteorite struck the Earth and its impact released large quantities of dust and vapour, which would have caused climate change on a global scale. Other theories suggest that a major volcanic eruption may have caused a great release of gases and ash. The result would have been a drop in world temperatures and the formation of acid rain. In the long term, the dust and ash could have led to a greenhouse effect (a warming-up of the layer of gases around Earth) that would have reduced the amount of sunlight reaching the Earth and caused many animals and plants to die.

LAYER OF IRIDIUM
The unusual amount of this rare element found in rocks dating from the end of the Cretaceous period supports the idea of a meteorite hitting the Earth.

BEE FOSSIL
Many groups of animals, including insects such as bees, managed to survive the destruction.

THE CHICXULUB CRATER

A crater in the Yucatán Peninsula, Mexico, was produced by a meteorite around 10 km (6 miles) in diameter that hit the Earth at the end of the Cretaceous period. Scientists believe this impact may have caused the extinction of the dinosaurs.

Mexico

Gulf of Mexico

Yucatán

Glossary

algae Organisms that live mostly in water and range from tiny forms to giant seaweeds.

amniote A creature with limbs and backbones that lays eggs; the category includes reptiles, birds and mammals.

amphibian A vertebrate animal that is adapted to live both on land and in water.

anatomy Structure of a living thing.

ankylosaur An armoured dinosaur from the early Jurassic and Cretaceous periods.

araucaria An evergreen coniferous tree, which has survived to modern times as a 'living fossil'. It is popularly known as a 'monkey puzzle tree'.

arthropod An invertebrate animal that has a hard, jointed outer skeleton. Arthropods include lobsters, crabs, spiders and centipedes.

asphalt A natural sticky, black liquid that is a form of petroleum. In some places it seeps from under the ground to the surface to form 'tar pits'.

bacteria Tiny, single-celled organisms that live in almost every environment on Earth.

bipedal Describes an animal that moves on two feet.

camouflage Body colours and patterns that allow animals to blend with their environment, making them difficult to spot.

canine teeth Long teeth at either side of the mouth, like fangs.

carnivore An organism that gets its main source of nutrition from animal flesh (a meat eater).

carrion Dead animals, often eaten by scavengers.

cartilage A flexible, elastic tissue that exists in the bodies of animals to connect joints and other parts.

cavity A hole. In fossils, it is a space inside or between bones that may indicate the size of organs or soft tissues that would have occupied it.

cephalopod Type of mollusc that lives in water and typically has arms or tentacles. They include squid, cuttlefish and octopuses.

ceratopsian A herbivorous, beaked dinosaur that flourished during the Cretaceous period, such as *Triceratops*.

cold-blooded Describes animals in which the body temperature varies according to the surrounding air temperature, such as fish.

conifer A tree with needle-shaped leaves and seeds attached to cones. Most conifers are evergreen (they do not shed all their leaves in autumn).

coprolites Fossilized faeces.

crop Birds, some dinosaurs and a few other animals have this pouch near the throat for the storage of food before digestion.

cycad A seed plant that typically has a woody stem with a crown of tough, evergreen leaves.

cynodont A mammal-like reptile that first appeared in the Late Permian period.

embryo The early stage of an animal while it is in the egg, or in the womb of its mother.

evolution The process of gradual change and adaptation of life forms over successive generations.

extinction The dying out of a species.

faeces Solid waste product from an animal.

fossil A trace of an organism that has been preserved from prehistoric times. Solid parts of animals, such as shells, teeth or bones, are changed over many millions of years into a stony substance in a process called 'fossilization'. Fossils may also be marks left behind by an organism, such as footprints, or faeces (coprolites), or patterns (impressions) left by skin texture.

gastrolith A stone deliberately swallowed by some animals in order to help grind up food in the digestive system. Some dinosaur fossils have been found with gastroliths.

gills Organs found in organisms that live in water, which allow them to 'breathe' by getting oxygen from the surrounding water, and excreting (giving out) carbon dioxide.

ginkgo A non-flowering tree that dates back around 270 million years, making it a 'living fossil'.

gizzard The muscular part of the stomach in birds and some other animals where food is broken down for digestion.

Gondwana Supercontinent of the Southern Hemisphere, which separated in the late Triassic period.

hadrosaur A duck-billed dinosaur belonging to the order Ornithischia.

herbivore An animal that obtains its nutrients from plants and other vegetation (a plant eater).

ice age Also known as a glacial age. A time in the Earth's geological history when global temperatures dropped, and large areas of the Earth's surface were covered by ice sheets. There have been several ice ages in Earth's history, some lasting for several million years. The most recent major ice age ended about 11,700 years ago.

ichthyosaurs A group of extinct reptiles that were adapted for life in water. They were abundant for much of the Mesozoic Era.

iguanodonts Herbivorous dinosaurs that included hadrosaurs and were widespread and very varied during the Cretaceous period.

invertebrate An animal without a backbone.

lambeosaurine A hadrosaur that had nasal passages that extended into the crest on the top of its head, such as *Lambeosaurus*.

Laurasia Supercontinent of the Northern Hemisphere, which separated in the late Triassic period.

ligament A tough band of tissue that holds together internal organs and connects bones in an animal or human body.

lungfish Air-breathing fish with one or two lungs.

mammal A warm-blooded vertebrate in which the young are fed with milk from the mother's mammary glands.

maniraptors A group that includes dinosaurs such as therizinosaurs and oviraptors, as well as birds.

marsupial An animal that carries its young in a pouch, such as a kangaroo.

membrane A thin layer of tissue that is often tightly stretched.

meteorite A natural object from space, such as a piece of rock, that hits Earth's surface. Most are vaporized by friction as they pass through Earth's atmosphere.

molluscs A large group of invertebrate animals that includes snails and slugs, as well as squid and octopuses.

neural spine Part of the vertebrae that, in some dinosaurs, became stretched into tall spines, which held up sails or humps of fat on their backs.

nutrients Vital substances obtained from food and needed for growth.

omnivore An organism that obtains its nutrients both from plants and other vegetation and from eating meat.

organism A life form, a living being.

Ornithischia One of the two main orders of dinosaurs (the other being Saurischia), based on the evolution of the hip bones into a birdlike hip structure. Birds themselves, however, are part of the order Saurischia.

ossify To harden like bone.

oviraptor One of a group of small theropod dinosaurs found in Mongolia. They included *Oviraptor* and *Caudipteryx*.

palaeontologist A scientist who studies the evidence of prehistoric life, for example fossilized remains.

Pangaea Supercontinent that included all Earth's continental masses at the beginning of the Mesozoic period.

phylogenetic tree A diagram that shows the evolutionary relationships between species or groups of species.

placoderms Early armoured fish.

plesiosaurs A group of extinct reptiles that were adapted for life in water.

pliosaurs Any of the short-necked plesiosaurs, such as *Liopleurodon*.

predator Any organism that hunts other organisms (its prey) for food.

pterosaur A flying reptile in which the forelimbs had evolved to create wings. Pterosaurs lived in the Mesozoic era.

quadruped An animal that moves about on four limbs.

reptile An amniote vertebrate that has scales covering its body. There are many extinct groups of reptiles, including the dinosaurs.

rhamphorhynchoids Pterosaurs that had beaked snouts, pointed teeth, and a long tail ending in a diamond-shaped flap of skin.

Saurischia One of the two main orders of dinosaurs (the other being Ornithischia), based on the evolution of the hip bones into a lizard-like hip structure. Birds belong to this order.

sauropodomorphs A group of long-necked, herbivorous dinosaurs that included *Plateosaurus*.

scavenger An animal that eats food killed or collected by other animals.

species In biology, a way of classifying a group of organisms that share characteristics and are capable of breeding with each other to produce healthy offspring.

spinal cord In vertebrates, the long bundle of nerves that connects the brain with the rest of the body.

stegosaurs A group of large, herbivorous armoured dinosaurs that included *Stegosaurus*.

supercontinent A single large landmass.

tendon A tough band of tissue that usually connects muscle to bone.

tetrapod A vertebrate with four limbs.

therapsids Mammal-like reptiles that include some ancestors of mammals.

therizinosaurs Dinosaurs that were originally meat eaters but then turned into herbivores.

theropods A group of mainly carnivorous dinosaurs that included *Tyrannosaurus rex*.

thorax In an organism, the middle region of the body between the head and the stomach.

titanosaurs A group of extremely large sauropod dinosaurs that included the biggest and heaviest creatures ever to walk on Earth, such as *Argentinosaurus*.

vertebrae The bones that form the backbone or spine.

vertebrate An organism with a backbone.

warm-blooded Describes animals, such as mammals and birds, in which the body temperature remains roughly constant and is controlled internally.

Index